LEADERS LEAD WHILE MANAGERS DICTATE

To my children, Jayden, Noah and Isabelle, the world is your playground, play well, play smart, have fun and make a difference. The world needs you as I need you.

To the world, it is with every word, the ability to open the mind of someone who never thought the power of words would enflame them to make the world their responsibility, one soul at a time. The truth exists, whether you run or hide. – Jason M. Ortiz

LEADERS LEAD WHILE MANAGERS DICTATE

WHAT YOU WILL GET FROM THIS BOOK

"Leaders Lead, Managers Dictate" is a book that not only gives detailed differences in the leadership that hurts communities and businesses but also the ones that inspire for optimal financial growth. There will be a series of everyday examples and tips that if utilized will guarantee growth in some manner that exceeds where you are standing today. I truly believe that implementation of true effective leadership will give a company growth and get them out of the position they stand in today.

You will get examples of what successful leaders who run billion dollar companies have done to make them stand out and continue to lead with workers who appreciate them. You will also learn how to motivate employees and others in ways that bring out their maximum in productivity and their willingness to go above and beyond the paycheck formulate.

Ultimately, if you are receptive enough to read this, you will be a better you and surround yourself with better leaders. Enjoy the journey and understand that Tougher Love is not punishment love, it's not a tough yelling type of love, it is a pure unadulterated ownership of your situation, type of love. People who want you to succeed will be honest with you every step of the way.

The Tougher Love series.

In the United States of America, disengagement with leaders and workers costs roughly 350 billion dollars annually. Studies have shown that roughly 30% of workers are fully engaged with their work and this is a direct impact from the disengagement they feel from leadership. There are 50% of workers just waiting to be engaged by leaders, waiting to feel acknowledgement so they can be inspired to give more than their paycheck requires. It is that direct engagement that is needed. There are 30% of workers that actively feel their supervisors do not even know their name or anything about them whatsoever. There are 60% of workers right now that admit to do what it takes to not get fired and have lost the initial desire that landed them at their place of work. Each one polled stated that the inadequate feelings they get from engagement or lack thereof from leadership was the main culprit.

WHAT IS A LEADER

In life leadership is important. Whether brokering deals, on the battlefield of war or even picking teams /teammates on a playground, leadership is important because leadership is a learned skill that when artfully embraced can influence and motivate people to do some amazing things.

Before going any further, let's establish what exactly is leadership. In the basic sense, leaders are simply people who lead, however, simply leading is not what a true leaders simply do, nor what an effective leader really does. Leaders are those that can get the best out of people. They set the tone in helping create a culture that is effective towards the goals and visions the leader strives towards. In business, the leader sets the tone, empowers and enforces the culture needed to not just bring out the best of all workers but to make sure that the company vision, the beliefs that keep the company afloat is core in each and every person on board. Leaders have the ability to make the vision become real and to motivate others to join in that transition. Leaders empower others. Leaders are everywhere; they are in communities, schools, and workplaces and even in your family. There are so much more and this book will offer you every important point that will help personally develop into leaders and/or your company to recognize leaders, hire leaders or create leaders to take your company further than it has been to this point. Only leaders can move you forward.

Leadership is about social influence; it is about goals, it is about vision and beliefs with an intended outcome.

People have a false sense of what leadership is and I think it is important to explain what leadership is NOT. Leadership is NOT seniority at some job. That just makes you a senior worker, a senior executive, NOT a leader. A leader is NOT a title, that is simply what a manager or supervisor has. Leaders are NOT automatically linked with ones personal attributes. People think leaders are loud and boisterous but that has absolutely nothing to do with leadership. Leadership is not about power, abuse and authority. Leaderships is NOT management, let me repeat for those that have been misled to believe such, LEADERSHIP IS NOT MANAGEMENT. They are not even remotely close. Leaders lead and managers dictate.

LEADERS SHOULD BE LIKED

I want to dive in with two amazing quotes about leadership and they are as follows:

"Leaders are people who do the right thing; managers are people who do things right."
–Professor Warren G. Bennis

"Leadership is the art of getting someone else to do something you want done because he wants to do it." – Dwight D. Eisenhower.

Do not think that leadership is something that people follow only because they have to get paid. This is not an effective method to productivity. A title such as manager or supervisor can easily produce this exact system. A management title only gets people to follow them because of title. They do not necessarily follow with passion or any purpose other than a weekly or bi-weekly check. They count down the days, they make sure they utilize company time going to the bathroom, walking slowly back to their desk, and the moment clock out time comes, they are already walking out the door. They enter lethargically and exit quickly. This is what happens when you have a title-based system that does not hold what you thought were leaders accountable for nothing more than the title of leadership. You cannot get the best but of people if all you have to offer is a title of leadership. Leadership must be more than a title. It simply must be.

Leaders should be liked. You don't have to compromise the company's vision or your morale to do this. Throughout the nation a large number of supervisors are not likeable and this happens most often in failing departments or where lawsuits are highest. You cannot lead someone you constantly antagonize and you constantly push around. Supervisors have no idea how many times workers see them and pretend not to see them to avoid engagement with them. This avoidance is not simply because of title but because of the type of leader you are or are not. You do not want to be labeled a douche bag or an asshole. Assholes and douche bags never get the full potential out of people, not anywhere near as much as an effective leader can.

In order to grow as an effective leader you have to be able to grow beyond your title. This does not mean you have to ignore or abandon your title, as a job must be performed. It is acknowledged that there are duties that must be adhered to but in order to get the optimal results out of workers, you must grow and be likeable beyond your title.

Try to remember that productivity and results are depending upon everyone, not just leadership. The entry-level people serve purpose as well. What is one way to get "lower level" workers to be incredibly productive? You produce by example. You show that you are in tune with their function and you make your presence felt by example. Stop by, engage and assist once in a while. In my work life, I have encountered very few leaders who were genuine and made me really want to go above and beyond for them. Most of the individuals in leadership roles were sitting on high horses, stealing ideas and taking credit for things they never did and even worse, at the expense of workers, tried to impress their superiors at the workplace. This of course damaged the morale of other workers. I do remember most vividly, the leader who was hands on and stood by my side in the most challenging of situations, valued my opinion and worked at the same problem synonymously with me and this made me give my all. This made me excited about returning the next day because there was hope at the workplace, because the vision, the belief that I had about being there in the first place was renewed and real again. One thing you have to take into account is that people will do what you show them more so than what you tell them. Leaders can do and they can say, people really like those who can do and say and do not like those that just dictate.

If you want to hire potential leaders, you need to know what a leader looks like. You need to be able to define the characteristics of an effective leader in order to know which person you are bringing into the organization will be an effective leader. Teaching someone what you know and not being able to do it is not as effective as teaching someone what you can actually do. You show, you talk through and then you pass it over to be demonstrated in return. You know this process is complete when you can show someone not only to do it successfully but to also train someone else to do it successfully and to develop leaders in the process. Great leaders develop great leaders who develop great leaders.

ARE YOU A PERSON DEVELOPER

Failed leaders send people to do things they have no idea about, but in order for your leadership to have any form of credibility that is even bigger than the manager title itself, you have to be able to attract those that are productive. This is infectious and trickles into your off work life as well. Attract who you are, not dictate who you want. If you want hard workers whom are willing to go above and beyond the call of duty, then you have to be that very person. You cannot successfully thrive and survive without being whom you want to attract.

You can attract leaders or those with potential to become leaders. Those with potential need to be developed a bit. Leadership is not something you are born with. People often confuse that with being aggressive, being outspoken and or being bossy. Leadership is a skill that is developed through beliefs, experience and the willingness to want to grow. Ask yourself this very question: are you a person developer? Can you develop people to become leaders and to become their most effective selves?

Developing people at a work place starts in the interviewing and hiring process. Leadership must be shown from the very start. Is the person, which is involved in the hiring and interviewing process doing it in an effective standard, and tone that develops the new hire? You need to have a clear image on what it is you want inside your company. The process can be frustrating, it can be time consuming but if done right, it will be rewarding.

An example of a good interviewer is when the interviewer not only expresses the vision and beliefs of the company but allows those being interviewed to express their vision and belief at the workplace and what characteristics they bring to the workplace. The interviewer should ask those being interviewed if they knew the difference between a manager/supervisor and a leader.

In the very beginning, leaders must try to get workers and potential workers ideas on the belief and vision of the company. A common vision and belief towards a common goal brings effectiveness, even if the individual assignment differs. Know in detail what it is that the worker's job entails. Take time to research and even make an attempt to physically understand it if applicable. One of the worst job interviews I have had was at a Hospital and the person interviewing me did not even know exactly what it was I would be doing if hired. They spoke randomly and when I asked questions, they made excuses and gave assumptions and I really did not want to give myself to such a mixed up and deceitful organization. This made a negative impact on me, and even though at that time I was not fully aware of all the details it took to be the most effective leader, I knew this was not one of them. The interviewer did not appreciate the interview process enough to be fully prepared and at a work place that is supposed to cater towards the well being of sick people, it is very important that leaders understand everyone's job functions that they are leading. They may not have to necessarily be experts at them but at least appreciate it enough to understand it. It was a turn off that I could not overcome. This was not a person developer, this was someone who gave off the stench of a manager that dictated and never appreciated.

Understand that all workers want to feel appreciated; they want to know that they matter. They want to know that their work matters, that they are more than a means of financial benefit to a company but also a part of something important. Workers will go above and beyond for a leader whom seems genuinely invested in the team concept and invested in the well being of the company as well as the workers and not just the company.

Too often workers, will do just their job, or enough of it to avoid being terminated, well, that's until they are completely burned out and end up doing something that causes a lawsuit or leads to termination. Look at the police department, Hospitals and rude customer service at other places of service and think about some of the rudest run-ins or even the ones that led to violence. These have been connected in some manner to a frustrated or burned-out worker who felt either disconnected from their management and or unappreciated. This all falls on leadership or lack thereof.

There is this guy named Roger. Roger is the team leader in this situation. Roger was hired by a company to lead a team of employees to win at a race for a benefit. Roger is fit and he is a runner by profession. The attainable goal here is to win the race in a timely manner, for each member on this team, all 5 of them, to reach that goal line.

During the race, John found that he was taking a step back while three other members of the team too a step forward. It was one of those feelings that set in where one began to question one's self. John was beginning to breathe heavier, he began to focus on that heavy breathing and the sweat that was trickling down and the finish line felt like it was further than it really was. Roger continued to look back and spurt encouraging words to the team to push them forward.

John began to realize that another worker was having just as hard a time as he was and John said to the other worker "Man, this is hard." The worker agreed and then said "I cant take it anymore, I'm ready to stop."

Now this hit John in two ways. The first way was that John now had a way out the race. John could simply agree with the worker and since the worker stopped, preventing the team from winning, John could stop right after and it would have no bearing on John whatsoever. John can continue to think that maybe if the other worker quits and the team loses, it is not John's fault. He can quit once the worker gives up and you will never be the loser of the team. John can hear him panting and huffing, puffing and gasping and the worker says to John, "I don't know if I can do it", John can easily say, "I know, me too". John does not have to assume leadership role to motivate the worker. John could easily refer to Roger and blame it on failed leadership or any other fictitious reason possible. This is de-motivating and leaders do not de-motivate. Now if you are thinking, Roger is the leader though, then you are right and wrong. Roger is the assigned team leader for the race but in every situation in life, whether work related or not, if other people are involved and a decision impacts others than yourself, you have an obligation as a decent human being to make decisions that benefit those that need it. It is what a leader would do.

Back to the story, how many of you reading this thought this was a good idea? How many of you would have taken this route? If so, then you are exactly what a leader is not. You need to develop the skills needed to move forward, to progress into the better you.

On the other hand, John thought that if they just stuck it out, as a team, the goal would be reached and then they not only would have done something great for a cause but also have done so together as a team. This would be able to trickle into the workplace and enforce a culture of teamwork and undying support for one another. If you only focus on the finish line and not the people in the race, you will have runners lag behind. You will find yourself in a position that you may have to get all the way to the back of the race and rebuild runners to try and merely catch up in a race you should be leading. Focus on people and you will see a team reach the finish line. This behavior helps develop others into leaders. This becomes infectious.

MOTIVATE EMPLOYEES

Ways to motivate employees.

First thing we have to do is understand that there are different types of motivation. There are the physical motivators that are connected in such that if you are thirsty, you are motivated enough to get up and get yourself a glass of water. If you are hungry, you may order or create a meal. There are also those that are motivated by monetary things. This of course are those that work for a paycheck or for a bonus or simply some form of monetary reward. Then there are those that are often overlooked and that's those that are motivated by what's fun, alluring and motivated because of their beliefs and vision. This is something that I have found myself to be more so than the rest although I am motivated in some ways by each and every one of those factors.

Most companies that do not exceed expectations and not do so because they are more focused on external methods such as monetary rewards and punishments and not in alignment with those that are motivated through common beliefs and vision, those that are genuinely interested and enjoy what they are doing. The old method is something that has been taught whether directly or indirectly and has been one that does not any longer sit well in today's society.

Nowadays, there has been too much influence through constant connection and people understand how many more opportunities and options they have, so they don't have to feel forced to live at a job and suffer for their entire lives just getting by paycheck to paycheck. You cannot grow a business successfully on that notion any longer, as there will be a wall you hit that you will not overcome unless your leaders motivate workers.

Here is a short list of things you can do to connect with workers that will ultimately motivate them.

1) Write to them. A personal, handwritten letter. Nothing says I appreciate you more that time invested into acknowledgement. To be able to sit for a moment and write to a worker why you appreciate them or that you have caught wind of something absolutely amazing they have done, this will not just induce great feelings from the worker but also will create an environment that is infectious. When having staff meetings, acknowledge the worker as well. Let everyone know that these great deeds/acts are synonymous with the company and that this is what leadership is about. People will chase the feel good acknowledgement with greater acts than they currently commit.

2) Show a genuine interest in your worker's after work lives. If you come across free information for children, send it out to them. For example, if you see something you come across about a circus coming to town with free tickets, you can simply send out a company email or post in common areas to all workers which simply states "For those with children, there are free tickets to the circus, you just have to log into…" Ask about long-term goals and follow up to show that you pay attention. Workers want to feel appreciated. If you have a worker whom is furthering their education or is working on a project, ask about it and then the next time you see them, follow it up with a light and simple "How's the project going?" or "How's school?" Very simple and incredibly effective.

3) Show interest in their other life situations. If a worker has to leave work early because of a family of health situation, follow up and ask how are things. Offer an ear or valid direction to an assigned ear in the department. Small gestures make a difference. A kind ear is never forgotten and can connect to a loyalty to the workplace that is needed to push forward towards a greater success.

4) Workers appreciate another worker/manager who listens. An attentive ear about possible ideas that could benefit the targeted population, the team and the company is a winning situation that should not be avoided. Leaders do not necessarily need to be the creator of the idea but the supportive ear of an absolutely winning idea. Workers will work hard for leaders who are invested in their well-being. I am very sure we have all at some point listened to someone else's idea and although we did not particularly agree with it, the idea they suggested led us to think about an even better one. Pay attention, you never know what success comes from an idea.

5) How much you express your acknowledgement and support of what workers do is important. Thousands of years ago, it was said to "do unto others as you would have done unto you", here we are thousands of years later and this holds as true as it ever did.

6) Do some cost effective, not so expensive ways to bond. Friday and Monday could be "coffee and a goal" days. Start the week with provided coffee and ask everyone to name a goal they wish to accomplish the week and follow up Friday to see if the goal was met. In companies that have thousands of employees, there are dozens of leadership figures that could be allocated to follow these fun

exercises that start the week motivating and end the week showing they are appreciated. Little things that can breed bonding and a connection that leads to more work.

7) Offer a new incentive for the worker that has the most praise from customers/clients/patients. If they park in the parking lot, offer a month free parking. If they take public transportation, offer a month transportation card. This is not an employee of the month, which you should already have, but some employees of the month have no, or limited engagement with customers, clients and/or patients. This added incentive would ultimately assist in creating an environment that lessens hostile interaction with customers and workers and pushes to show how much the dialogue of positive engagement is appreciated by leadership.

8) Set up a system that emails every worker on their registered birthday to show them they are remembered, appreciated and honored on their birthday. If you have a smaller amount of workers you can even celebrate everyone's birthday for the month on a designated day with a potluck or a small gathering to exchange pleasantries.

There are things that will not motivate as much as managers think. Some of these presently used failed motivators actually lead to more problems at the workplace. What needs to be known and understood is that optimal motivation will not come from simply employee of the month or punishment methods. Incentives cannot only be when an employee does exceptionally well but there has to be a consistency in acknowledgement all the way throughout the process.

Studies show that the negative/positive incentive approach is hopeless and does absolutely nothing for motivation in the long run. Incentives can be good but it cannot be a sole motivator. There has to be a culture of acknowledgement that breeds inspiration. The great leaders know how to inspire workers to rally behind the cause and the beliefs of the leader and the company/agency they work for.

You want workers that work beyond mere incentives and paychecks? Then you have to inspire workers to appeal to their higher value, their beliefs, and the belief that their work matters and that it impacts the targeted population in which they serve. Bonuses are often given at particular workplaces and there is a consensus that those that receive it or not necessarily the best workers. Bonuses do not appeal to the worker whom is passionate about the commonality of belief the company has with their values. Bonuses will not get workers to believe in the company's mission and values. Now, I am not saying remove the bonus system as workers need money but there are other methods to get more out of workers.

You have to create a vision that inspires workers to buy into the vision of the company. Have them be proud of what they do. People want to feel as if they serve a purpose to humanity and the workplace is no different. Research any information that links workers to a greater cause and you will find things like a nurses impact, a retail experience that helped someone, a kind bus driver and so many other examples. People become more motivated when being able to contribute to a cause that matters/inspires them. Let them know you understand their role and that their role is impactful. Workers cannot be disconnected from the company's vision because then they will not buy into the systematic approach or to changes and they will ultimately just simply do "their job" and nothing more.

As a leader, you have to create a cohesive unit. Being hired for a job may seem to be enough but it is not. Motivation must be a continuous process and must be something that is cultural. The companies' and leader's value must be expressed in a manner that sells to workers something they can buy into. Putting up notes that probably had no damn thought into it on some cluttered bulletin board does not sell enough.

If you create a thoughtless environment by not being thoughtful, you will find workers whom feel they are underappreciated and being pulled from many directions. These feelings lead to chaos, which leads to lawsuits and this can all be avoided. Workers can feel pulled in every direction or needed in more than one place because they are valued. You decide which one it can be. Your decision will either lessen productivity and breed to a culture of problems that will be hard to break or productivity will flourish and the culture will lead to success.

ATTITUDE EQUALS INCOME

It is important to understand the concept of "Attitude Equals Income" and this simply means that ones attitude will determine the amount of income or lack of income that is generated to the corporation/business. The attitude of the culture will be one of the driving forces behind how profitable your business will be or has been. Effective leaders help workers feel great about themselves and their purpose at work. This attitude translates to productivity, which must also be acknowledged, as it will create a cycle of productivity and positivity at the workplace.

If you can change one's attitude, you will be able to lessen lawsuits and increase the most productive environment. It starts with leadership and must be infectious all the way down. I have witnessed and I am sure we all have or have seen it on the news, the moment the worker with the attitude caused all sorts of ruckus that led to a decline in sales and a hefty lawsuit that could have been prevented. Do not ever think the only infectious attitude is a positive one. Negativity has the same power to be infectious as positivity so it is imperative that leaders are effective and take heed to everything I have written in this book.

ADDITIONAL SKILLS

Communication skills are a leaders greatest weapon. It is the lack of these skills that can bring forward the dictator within and this will lead to problems when managing employees while trying to get the maximum out of workers. The reality in the role of manager/employee is that the leader is selling self and the system to workers. It is in the hands of the leader to be a great communicator to get the message across effectively without attitude imposing its will and distorting the message from its original mission. How does one do such? Well here a few keys that could help:

Be clear when you communicate. Always remember that how you think the message is sent out is not necessarily how the worker perceives it. Ask for clarity, make sure workers understand what it is that you are disseminating. If misinterpretation sets in due to quick and unclear communication, then productivity fails.

How many times have we encountered workers who believe certain rules exist that do not exist? How many times has the wrong advice been given due to information being taken differently and unclearly? It is not because they believe they are wrong, it is because the way they share the information is how they perceived it when they received it.

Be true to yourself and be authentic. How real are you about who you are? Some people tend to pull back their own values or their beliefs because they want to agree or fear they cant get workers on board with the plan. Fake smiles do not work at all. People will see how fake you are and ultimately, your path to motivate and inspire also comes across as fake. Needless to say how much productivity you miss out on with being fake.

Be assertive. Body language images and words all serve purpose. You may not be the best speaker but you have to find a balance that your assertiveness is not taken any way less than serious. Insistence and persistence are partners to assertiveness. Don't concern yourself with whether or not workers will mistake assertiveness for rudeness. You know the line that you shouldn't cross and you have to be aware of your assertiveness not to cross that line. Do not pull back from being assertive because you think workers will not want to comply. They know the structure and the system and they will comply with your assertive position as long as lines to rudeness are not crossed. Being offensive is not being assertive neither as you have to really make sure you are strong but not bullying.

Be someone who is viewed as an open-minded person This means that you are willing to accept other's points of views for the better of the organization and that it is not only about you. Those that do not embrace open-mindedness and dogmatic, they impress upon workers that they are not someone they can go to and they are not trust worthy nor in any position to be a communicator. Closed-minded supervisors fail at being effective leaders. Alternative ideas and scenarios are educational to everyone at some point. People have different cultures and life experiences and their point of view may be enlightening. Do not rob the relationship of effective leader - worker by being close-minded. Workers tend to avoid contact with close-minded supervisors. You don't have to like the idea that is being said to you but if you are an intelligent person, you can stay there and listen because you know how much each listening moment plants the seed to a greater communication and more productivity at work.

Be a listener. This is something that goes a long way. Communication is not just talking. How many times has there been a meeting when the leader talked extensively and when the worker wanted to speak back, there was not an engaging dialogue. I am very sure we all have engaged with the person who only listens waiting to respond and not actually at what is being said to them. This is a recipe for disaster. When it comes to work related matters, the stakes are too high. Production is important and you will not ever know where the direct problem lies if you do not listen. Ask yourself, which of these need improvement. Focus on each one until you see improvement. Keep notes on your improvement and make it a part of your daily routine.

Be empathetic. The other person wants to feel like they are being heard and understood. A worker who believes that "leadership gets me, they understand" tend to be more productive that the worker who works harder only in the presence of the leader and slacks the moment the leader walks away. This is cultural; this starts with leadership impact or lack thereof and tends to be harder to remove than expected.

MISTAKES LEADERS MAKE

Although this section is entitled "Mistakes leaders make", the reality is, leaders whom have acquired the skill, whom have practiced improvement and taken into account the most important aspects of leadership would not make these mistakes, these are manager and supervisor mistakes. Leaders have already evolved and grown from the title itself.

Attitude is huge when it comes to leadership and workers whom are not in supervisory roles. It is important that leaders understand that displaying the wrong attitude has a trickled down effect on the stalling productivity and the stalling of the growth of the company. Leaders must never display arrogance. An act of arrogance sets a tone with workers that are hard to alter. Some people already assume their supervisor is going to be a hard-nosed prick that just gives orders and dictates without understanding as it is. You never want to reinforce that notion whatsoever. A supervisor should never confuse his individual success with the success of the team and never act as if he is the reason the company stays afloat without remembering all that everyone does. The level of social distance and mistrust that becomes formulated can never be mentioned enough as this damages morale and motivation amongst workers.

Leaders should never lose track of the values in which they hold. They should never compromise them for petty gains and at the expense of others. A leader that talks about value but does not show any that can be respected or commendable is not one that will get the most of out their workers. Some leaders lack value while others on a different end of the spectrum have been consumed with a vision. Now normally this sounds like a key to success and in some way it is, but not at the expense of the workers. The vision of the company should be a common belief and imbedded in the culture of the company and something that most if not, all the workers share.

One major mistake that supervisors/directors/managers do is that they put their self-interests ahead of the interests of the company/agencies they operate. The problem is they are only looking out for their own position of power, their own false sense of fame and glory and their own money and this in some form hurts the economic position of the company.

Another mistake that is made by those in leadership roles is their position of certainty and close-mindedness. These individuals are unwilling to evolve with time and change for the greater of the company and the workers in which they employ. This is connected to everything being about them. When certainty becomes the mindset, then this particular type of leader does not seek to grow or to learn more, stumping their growth and the growth of the company. A wise man once said, "The only thing that never changes is the fact tat everything changes" and this holds true to all forms of business. Look at the evolution of technology. The unwillingness to progress becomes an expense to those workers whom the company drives off of. This ultimately leads to another mistake, which is breaking trust. What people fail to realize in their hunt for money and power is that no one can get to success alone. Bill Gates did not, Steve Jobs did not and you will not. There is always someone connected to your journey and workers whom are waking up early and working good hours to ensure that your product is quality. No one person can be the great success story alone and this is a mistake of leadership roles.

LEADERS MUST ENGAGE WITH TEAM MEMBERS

In the United States of America, disengagement with leaders and workers costs roughly 350 billion dollars annually. Studies have shown that roughly 30% of workers are fully engaged with their work and this is a direct impact from the disengagement they feel from leadership. There are 50% of workers just waiting to be engaged by leaders, waiting to feel acknowledgement so they can be inspired to give more than their paycheck requires. It is that direct engagement that is needed. There are 30% of workers that actively feel their supervisors do not even know their name or anything about them whatsoever. There are 60% of workers right now that admit to do what it takes to not get fired and have lost the initial desire that landed them at their place of work. Each one polled stated that the inadequate feelings they get from engagement or lack thereof from leadership was the main culprit.

Let me make this clear for those who think that all it takes is some action plan or some survey to fix the issue of employee engagement, if you think that is the solution, you've already lost revenue. This usually leads to some 3 day course at work that leaves supervisors and workers mislead and confused and after two weeks of implementation of whatever action plan you think is going to work, it all falls apart and reverts back to the same distance and lack of productivity that is already plaguing the workplace.

A worker who is actively engaged by leadership is on average 30-40% more productive any day of the week than their disengaged counterpart. That level of productivity not only comes with creativity and passion but also reduces the amount of lawsuits that lack of productivity or just trying to get by creates. Every work place can encounter a worker who is known as a slacker, an opportunist and/or non-productive. It is at these times, that a leader should not distance themselves and wean out the possible distraction but instead engage with them, find out what motivates them and inspire them to be more productive. Some companies that do not see them most profit have the biggest turnover ratio of employee hires. They feel that people who do not produce at the expected level is not just a problem but not fixable. This is the cultural mindset that trickles down to other workers whom only see the threat of termination and not the opportunity for growth.

Great leaders have both emotional and engagement intelligence. This is something that requires leaders to take time to understand the workers, the culture of the workplace and to know what are their motivators. The threat of termination is not an effective motivator as this only produces workers to find ways to evade termination but not ways to work beyond the paycheck. This creates the atmosphere of the "That is not my job description", "I don't get paid to do that", "That's not my problem" kind of culture which evidently leads to less profit, more lawsuits and dissatisfied customers.

Create a culture of engagement; people have the need to feel important in some manner, even if for a moment in a day. You have to declare that not only is employee engagement going to happen but also that it is imperative and that you will take responsibility for it. This is something all in leadership roles must implement and make a norm within the culture.

A problem with many companies is that they do not celebrate any contributions of success that leadership and executives can't take glory for; instead they are too busy giving attention and making threats of termination or demotion when errors occur. This creates a culture of mistrust, deceit and a series of employees who will do just enough to not have these negatives be pushed upon them. They will simply do enough to continue receiving a check without caring about the overall organizations beliefs or goals because when leadership does not engage, these goals and beliefs become myths and lies that are used to lure in workers. The common worker is not a moron, they often apply for two reasons, they need a job and the job they apply for is one they are attracted to within. What happens in the course of time when employees lose their passion for the belief of the company often is a direct correlation with how leadership treats workers. The attitude of leadership trickles down to the worker whom is most responsible for the success of your company. Never lose focus of that truth.

Let me makes this as clear as can be….. Whenever someone receives acknowledgement, a good compliment about their performance, they will perform better to seek another. The passion to connect with humans is one that is underestimated and overlooked dramatically, so much so that it cost companies billions a year in revenue losses.

Let me give an example of what we do as humans, a drug user gets a particular high off of a drug that they feel at that time is absolutely amazing, they will seek that feeling. SO WILL YOUR WORKER. The engagement and acknowledgement is something that continues to drive passion and begins in the hiring process all the way through to retirement and beyond.

If you make someone feel great about themselves, they will feel a sense of loyalty to you and to your cause. They will go above and beyond to make sure that your goals and the belief of the company is pushed forward.

Ask employees questions that matter. Many times surveys are filled with generic questions that offer generic answers and are incorporated in systems that make employees feel unsafe to answer honestly. Ask real questions like "What are you most satisfied with at work?" "When was the last time you feel incredibly motivated at work and what motivated you?" "What needs to happen at work for you to feel appreciated?" "How valued do you feel by leadership?" "How valued do you feel by customers?" These questions will show you what is needed to get the absolute most productive selves out of them. Be unafraid to hear truth and to hear something you may not like. It is for the greater of the relationship and for company productivity.

Successful people find what they are individually good at, where as successful leaders find what others are good at. How does this happen? By following the few keys to being an effective leader. These keys are communication and listening, being true to self and being assertive.

Improve staff morale. Emphasize employee engagement. Raise accountability as you raise engagement but you have to lead by example. Send notes to employees to specifically show their contribution is acknowledge and important to the company. If a customer or patient says something good about a worker, jot down a short hand written note thanking the worker for being an integral part of the team. The goal is to increase sales, satisfaction and the reality is attitude equals income, whether by addition or subtraction. A leader should show that he/she pays attention to workers.

Inspiring action from workers is not from dictatorship; it is not from the threat of punishment or from belittling workers by yelling at them, nor will inspiring action from workers come from embarrassing them in front of other co-workers, it comes from the purpose, belief and the way we communicate with workers.

People will buy into why you do something more so than what you do. When it comes to the ability to drive behavior, statistics, facts, information's, benefits and features will not inspire action. When you speak to workers from within, from the inside going out, you are speaking in the direction of the brain that controls behavior and that's deep inside. People will be inspired by beliefs and by something they can buy into. Numbers, statistical data and figures do not have that driving force, it just simply cannot inspire like speaking to ones moral compass, their beliefs can.

Have you ever seen data, or heard data and something in your gut tells you that something about it does not feel right? That gut feeling is where inspiration lies.

An example I love as an effective leader is the CEO of Starbucks, Howard Schultz.

CEO of Starbucks, Howard Schultz, is known to invest in other people's success as well as his own. He is known to be hard driven and yet a great leader. Starbuck is known for the positive manner in which employees and customers are treated, with customers being called the name they wish to be called and not just sir or ma'am. Starbucks offers benefits such as insurance and that is not excluded to part-time workers. In 1997, there was a robbery in one of the locations that led to three employees being killed in Washington D.C. CEO Howard Schultz did not go the politically correct route, he did not focus on sales, but instead he Instead flew to Washington D.C. and spent the week with the employees and their families in the area. This is the type of leadership that was needed for workers and this trickled down as this was the culture and the way things were done from the top all the way down. Schultz's compassion and courage has never gone overlooked. He boldly and effortlessly showed how much the value of the workers meant to him, even over numbers.

Over the past five years Jim Sinegal has shepherded his company Costco to impressive returns. Costco's stock has doubled, and revenues continue to grow at an impressive rate.

Yet Sinegal might be better known as a man of the people at Costco. His nametag plainly says "Jim," he answers his own phone, and his plain office at the company headquarters doesn't even have walls. While other CEOs are spending tens of thousands of dollars just decorating their offices, Sinegal's pays himself a yearly salary of $350,00. Most CEOs of large company are paid in the millions. His simple contract is only a page long, and even includes a section that outlines how he can be terminated for not doing his work.

So how did he come up with that number? He figured he shouldn't be paid more than 12 people working on the floor.

His employee turnover rate is the lowest in the retail industry, over *five times less* than rival Wal-Mart. In an age where CEOs are paid in the millions and would never be seen in the "trenches," Jim Sinegal is an anomaly. And his workers love him for it.